THE BOOK OF
THE BOOK

Books by Idries Shah

Sufi Studies and Middle Eastern Literature
The Sufis
Caravan of Dreams
The Way of the Sufi
Tales of the Dervishes: *Teaching-stories Over a Thousand Years*
Sufi Thought and Action

**Traditional Psychology,
Teaching Encounters and Narratives**
Thinkers of the East: *Studies in Experientialism*
Wisdom of the Idiots
The Dermis Probe
Learning How to Learn: *Psychology and Spirituality in the Sufi Way*
Knowing How to Know
The Magic Monastery: *Analogical and Action Philosophy*
Seeker After Truth
Observations
Evenings with Idries Shah
The Commanding Self

University Lectures
A Perfumed Scorpion (Institute for the Study of Human Knowledge and California University)
Special Problems in the Study of Sufi Ideas (Sussex University)
The Elephant in the Dark: *Christianity, Islam and the Sufis* (Geneva University)
Neglected Aspects of Sufi Study: *Beginning to Begin* (The New School for Social Research)
Letters and Lectures of Idries Shah

THE BOOK OF THE BOOK

Idries Shah

The value of the dwelling
is in the dweller.
Saying

ISF PUBLISHING

Contents

Preface

A LIONESS, ACCORDING to Aesop, was asked by some other
animals how many cubs she produced at one birth.
She said:

"One – but that one is a lion."

Idries Shah

1

The Dervish Who Became a King

There was once a dervish who had seen Truth.

He decided that he would have to become powerful in the ordinary world before people would listen to him, so he applied all his concentration to the task of attaining visible authority.

In the course of time he became a king.

When he had spent some time as a ruler, the dervish realized that people did not want his way of teaching.

They appeared to hear him, but acted only from hope of reward or fear of punishment.

This dervish-king lacked an instrument with which to teach.

None came to him until he was almost at the end of his days.

2

The Stranger Dressed in Green

One day the aging king, out on a hunting
   expedition, had sat down to rest when a
   stranger, dressed in green, approached.
Saluting the king he told him a story, this story,
   The Tale of the Book.
The next Section begins the Tale of the Book.

3

Contrary to Expectation

A wise man, the wonder of his age, taught his
   disciples from a seemingly inexhaustible store of
   wisdom.
He attributed all his knowledge to a thick tome
   which was kept in a place of honor in his room.
The sage would allow nobody to open the volume.
When he died, those who had surrounded him,
   regarding themselves as his heirs, ran to open
   the book, anxious to possess what it contained.
They were surprised, confused and disappointed
   when they found that there was writing on only
   one page.
They became even more bewildered and then
   annoyed when they tried to penetrate the
   meaning of the phrase which met their eyes.
It was: "When you realize the difference between
   the container and the content, you will have
   knowledge."

4

The Opinion of the Scholars

The successors to the sage took the book to the
    most famous scholars of the times, saying:
"We have this book, and seek your interpretation.
It belonged to such-and-such a sage, the wonder of
    the age, now dead.
This is all he left behind, and we are unable to
    fathom its mystery."
At first the scholars were delighted to see a work
    of such size, bearing the name of its former
    owner, whom they knew to have been revered
    by multitudes of people.
They said:
"We will of course give you the real
    interpretation."
But when they found that the book was all but
    empty, and what words there were made no
    sense to them, they first sneered and then
    shouted at the students, driving them away in
    their fury.
They believed that they had been victims of a
    hoax.
That was a time when scholars were limited and
    literal-minded.
They could not imagine a book which could *do*
    something, only a book which *said* something.

5

The Interpretation of the Dervish

The dispirited students, going to rest in a
    caravansary, came upon a dervish, and told him
    of their perplexity.
He said:
"What did you learn from the scholars?"
The travelers said:
"Nothing. They could tell us nothing."
The dervish said:
"On the contrary, they told you everything.
They showed that the book was not to be
    understood in the manner assumed by you, or
    by them.
You may think that they lack depth.
But you, in your turn, lack sense.
The book was teaching something through the
    incident itself, while you remained asleep."
But the students found this explanation too subtle
    for their minds, and the only person who
    maintained the knowledge of the book was a
    casual visitor to the caravansary, who overhead
    the interchange which I have just repeated to
    you, O King and Dervish!
The stranger dressed in green then stood up and
    walked away.

6

The Guarding and
Theft of the Book

The king was so impressed by the stranger's story
that he ordered the story to be inscribed and
bound in a large book.

This was placed in a niche in his treasury and
guarded by armed men, day and night.

The aged king died and a barbarian conqueror
devastated his realm.

Breaking into the treasury, this man saw the book
in its place of honor and said to himself: "This
must be the source of the country's happiness,
wisdom and prosperity."

He said aloud: "Let the book be taken down and
read out to me in our own language."

But this conqueror, for all his physical power, was
an ignoramus; he could make no sense from the
words in the book.

7

Mali Saves the Book

The barbarian had the book destroyed, but his
  interpreter, whose name was Mali, remembered
  its contents.
It is through his work that its teaching was passed
  down. Mali opened a shop.
He kept copies of *The Book of the Book* on view,
  for sale.
Nobody was allowed to look inside until he had
  paid two gold pieces for a copy.
Some learned the lesson of the book, and came
  back to study with Mali.
Others wanted their money returned, but Mali
  always said:
"I cannot give you back your money until you
  return me what you have learned from the
  transaction, as well as the book itself."
Some who preferred mere appearance to inner
  content, called Mali a deceiver.
But Mali told them: "You were, all along, seeking
  deceivers, so you will assume that you have
  found one in anyone."

8

Yasavi Buys It for Twelve Gold Pieces

When Ahmed Yasavi was a student, he bought a
copy of The Book from Mali, paying two gold
pieces.
The following day he returned, and gave Mali
another ten pieces of gold, saying: "What I have
learned from The Book is worth more than this.
But since I have no more money I give it all to
you, in token of my valuing this lesson as equal
to my entire possessions."

9

Yasavi of the Masters Transmits It

Yasavi had the history and the content of *The
  Book of the Book* bound in a volume of over
  two hundred pages, on whose cover was
  written:
  "If the thickness of books determines the value
  of their content, this one should assuredly be
  even thicker."
Since Ahmed Yasavi, of the Masters of Central
  Asia, this story has been transmitted for more
  than seven hundred years.